Poetry

For the

Now

Johan Lewis

iUniverse, Inc.
New York   Bloomington

Poetry For the Now

*The views expressed in this work are solely those of the author
and do not necessarily reflect the views of the publisher, and
the publisher hereby disclaims any responsibility for them.
iUniverse books may be ordered through booksellers or by contacting:*

*iUniverse
1663 Liberty Drive
Bloomington, IN 47403
www.iuniverse.com
1-800-Authors (1-800-288-4677)*

*Because of the dynamic nature of the Internet, any Web addresses or
links contained in this book may have changed since publication and
may no longer be valid. The views expressed in this work are solely those
of the author and do not necessarily reflect the views of the publisher,
and the publisher hereby disclaims any responsibility for them.*

*ISBN: 978-1-4401-1600-1 (pbk)
ISBN: 978-1-4401-1601-8 (ebk)*

Printed in the United States of America

iUniverse rev. date: 1/19/2009

For the genius. Again?

LIVID

Down the sad stretch of highway,
Lays a little naked boy.
Sucking his thumb and twiddling his lips
He is alone.
Tornado, Tornado.

Juxtapose his girth
With a sigh of relief,
And he will live again.

TUBE OF DELIGHT

Dangling from the fairy-dock,
Time stands free.
Transcending through the stillness
Is the breast of iniquity.

And when we look upon her,
She smiles back.
And shakes our twisted edges
And pervades the now.

DELUSIONAL SELF

Understand it, and it will undermine you.
Defeat it, and it will overcome you.

Beaming down the barrel of my youth
Is my desire for the notion of a fixed point–
Why do I need to define?
Shooting out my youth,
My years grow on me and circle me.
Is it all too late?
Or is the now accepting of late entries?
I wonder
If you need me.
Do you need me?
Or are you just using me?

Tell me, dearest, because I am dying from the past…

WINDOW

A glass plate between you and I
What is it called?
The difference between touch and separation
What is it called?
Layers and layers of love
Labored strong by dwarves of passion,
And doves of justice.

Is it right that only light or brute force
Can pass through?
Why can it not be
A way I can get to you?

FALLING TVs

Transcending light for my plight,
Understand what moves me.
As it falls closer to you
Wrap your face around it.

Godly hours beam down
And burn our human skin
But others point and laugh
When I smile
And know there's something
More to this place.

FROSTY WEATHER

Mystify me,
And follow me through the fields,
The oil is burning
And the hour is now.
Our sweat coated hands hold forever
The key to our extinguishment
And yet all we have are gates to heaven.

ESSENCE

With or without a father,
The telephone rings.
The other line is not as straight
And pierces my mind.

Pants upon Pants.
Palm Hotel.
Room 4-something-something.
The dream displays mighty wit,
And awakens a waiting for nothing happening.
Grow what you feel and
Know what you must
But the end result is mist.
Clear nothing away.
Uncertainty is human.

COMPETITION

Confuse my being with an animal,
And bats will talk nonsense.
Violins playing sexual songs,
Piercing the virginity of silent composers.
Water flows down a tunnel
And fire hydrants beam their incoherence.
The winner undetermined,
Leaning towards the lesser,
What is winning
What is now
Who are you?
Be me.
What are we?

PHILOSOPHY

A flush, a straight, a naked woman.
Hello Wednesday night poker.
Smokey confessions from a baby
In a sticky, leathery lounge chair
He says, "Change me!"
And I say, "Call!"

SHUTTING DOWN

When a ram chunk of chunk factor five
Shoots your way,
Hit it out of the park.
Cause when that ball is sailing free,
It is then that you find pervading serenity.
Chunk your troubles away
And ram them apart.
And when the ram chunk,
Chunk factor five,
Comes barreling down,
Show it a chunk factor of SIX,
And laugh in your victory.

UNAWARE

Linking together our pasts of fury
With the glue of poverty
Breeds destruction and lust.
Distance the truth from fact
And fiction from real.

Whip cream suits me well.

The lines of justice
Are drawn with the pens of land owners
And those who are lifeless
Are those who borrow

Can I have almonds on that?

Up on a high mountain
The rain does not fall easily
In the valley it floods the blood
Of a pharaoh.

Two scoops, please.

And put a cherry on it. Now.

SKY–CYCLE

Like the sleep before waking,
Ambient mist in the morning light
Alludes me to wake.

Rumble bumble rumble bumble

Awake.
And as the plates shatter
Underground,
A spider will crawl
As powerful as Stone Henge.

And when the sun sets,
The sky crawls into bed,
The moon reads a nighttime story
About stars looking up to men
For inspiration.
As for now, I look up
And see my father.

THE LONGING OF SIR AL–AMUD DE LA TORRE

Look at that lake, son.
It breathes melancholy.
Whence does it fall on soft ears?
Loose lips on the bows of truth
Notwithstanding what we know,
Cannot feel the irony of a jar.

And when the youth of pigeons
Feel the inside of tomorrow's wealth,
It is a marginal feeling indeed.

Trapped inside I feel your longing.
Are you there?
Please say so.
Because I'm tied to a heavy weight
And the river is running higher.

PEACE AND RESUR–SECTION

Shine the call of drunken masters,
And feel the night encircling your head.
Pump it, pump it,
Goes the lark,
And trials may be needed
By fire?

It calls any who speak
The utters of the few
And shuns the desires of the wicked.

For when it is un-time
Those who are not prepared will
Fail under the blasters
And corpses
And beetles
And dung heaps
And wizards
And reptiles
And fiords
And dandelions
And marsupials
And hobos
And Presidents.

LOOKING THROUGH LIFE–TINTED GLASSES

Turn round and round until death,
While the Reaper pops his mouth on the rocks.
A jab of lightning,
A punch of power,
A bout to the clouds.

Sway back and north,
Confusion is my little son.
Hang me out to dry,
For the season is here.

Amongst the reeves a rat conspires
And a child is lost.
And the now
Reigns.

DEFEATED EVOLUTION VIS A VIS POONDADDY

Tempest, you dream too soon,
Orlando is not near enough.
Feel the warm coast beneath your sheets
You bore.
Will you tempt me again, noble steed?
Or will you kick off maladies that will truly be your
vengence?

The fire is near!
The fire is soon!
The fire dreams of Cancun!

The sand in your toes crunches me,
Words are written down to you in the most cursory of
ways,
You are undeserving of my senile praise.
With arms wide open I welcome your torrent,
The island girls behind me run for their suckling pig.
What is ritual, and what is form?
Can you feel the mountains tremble?

The fire is near!
The fire is soon!
The fire sings to a different tune!

Embellish around me,
Do what you do best and it is enough,
The now will swallow you whole
Inside the girth of Man's fate.
Do I move you?
Do you quake with firm stability?
Haughty eyes undress you
And the rain is a gift.

The fire is near!
The fire is soon!
The fire is just another moon!

Pass me by and find out years later
That you ruined houses, but not mine!
No, not mine!
Men into swine? How low can you go!
Orlando is close; he has been warned!

I finally enter you with assured grace…
And we are both two as one,
And you say you need my thesaurus.

Well, sorry, I left it at home.

"TIME" TRANSLATES TO "PAIN" IN PIGLATIN

Center your mind around a fixed pole
And swing it around: mental tetherball.
Three, crust, seven, apple, two, zero, three again,
Numbers and pie: a duality in the baking.
Now it's time to die and live, monk–
Eat your banana,
Take my head off and rest it on the gate,
For France is free!
Tanks of love with shells of screaming salesmen,
And you're the diver
My jungle boogie queen.
Steer your vessel through the mud
(Gosh, your toes are freezing!)
Can you please drive straight?
We're finishing a revolution,
And I have to be a backseat tank driver.
Load, click, bang.
Kiss.
I love Paris in the summer with you, Army Margaret.

SHOWDOWN AT THE NO–KAY CORRAL

My beard of bees,
Is better than your slippery cock.

PEACETIME IN RUSSIA

Why is it that reality wins
When it is placed up against the whore of night?
Why do dreams show
What we cannot do?
Offer them a bagel
With butter,
And they will give you back a quarter,
Those little beggars.

THE OLD WAY

Flail and file your files
And out away the dates
You think you had.
Find a way to
Circumcise a goat,
And I will give you my inheritance.

PACIFIC CONFESSIONS

In the old time there lived a fox,
Who leapt from tree to tree,
And in the coffee shops of his mind he saw a girl,
Red haired and fruitful.
And when he leapt from the coffee shop tree
To the skyscraper tree,
He left nothing in question.
One was one,
And that was that.
No lines of gray
To fiddle with in his life.

But gorges are hard to avoid,
Even if you're a fox.
And a slip of the paw
Brings down even the cleverest.

And down the fox fell,
Into the valley,
Where there lived no coffee shops,
No skyscrapers stood,
And no red haired girls danced.
Into a world he went, stranger than his own
And he was filled with ecstasy and mystery.
And when the bottom he reached,
A monster came to him.

"Where do you come from?" said the monster.
"Please do not kill me," replied the fox.
"Kill you? Ha ha!" laughed the monster. "I mean not
To kill you, little fox."
The fox sighed a great sigh, and went
To shake the monster's giant hand.

And the monster extended a baby hand,
And they shook.
The monster procured a small ham,
And they both ate in peace,
Talking about their families,
And how stressful the holidays had been.
"I know," said the monster.
"I was like, *who* is sleeping in my room tonight?"
And they both laughed.

But out of the bushes came
A pleasant little sheep.
And the fox smiled: the cuteness was overwhelming.
And the sheep charged!
And the monster screamed and leapt in the air!
And oh how the sheep spread its wings
And flew towards the monster
And used its razor fangs to take it down,
And ripping into the carcass, the sheep stared at the
shaking fox,
Who was looking at the mangled body of the monster,
And was crippled with fear,
And the sheep walked calmly over, his green eyes
glowing,
And said, "You are not a monster.
I will leave you alone.
Climb this ladder, and go back to your world."
And out of the sky came a ladder that
Lead to nowhere.
It slammed to the ground with a thud.
When the dust settled,
The fox looked up at the sheep with
Fear,
And climbed the ladder.

After twenty or so pegs, the
Fox looked down.
The sheep had picked up the
Monster's carcass in its talons
And started to fly it across the land,
The large claws and horrible face
Limply bobbing up and down
Towards the horizon.
The fox looked at the rest of the ladder,
And it seemed to go to nowhere.
He looked back at the monster,
And thought of its genteel demeanor.
And their pleasant conversation,
And decided that enough was enough,
That no one takes a stand anymore,
That all the other foxes he had known
Were cowards,
And he couldn't go back to the
Dancing red haired girl
Without standing for a little justice.

And he called out to the sheep,
"You who are not worthy of
such a majestic food!
Come back and stand with me, and
I will fight you!
I will avenge the gentle giant
That you have slain unfairly!"

And the sheep looked back,
Its innocent face scowling, and dropped the carcass
Of the monster
And hundreds of feet it hurled down,
Gaining momentum, and
Crushed a villager's cottage
With a large and dusty cloud of destruction.

And the sheep flew to the peg
Where the fox was,
Floating next to him, flapping its leather wings
That spanned five meters,
And said, "Do you see
What happens when you open your mouth,
Fox?
More have died needlessly.
You should not have meddled in this world.
Death comes to you now."

And out of the sheep's chest
Sprang a tentacle with a head of a small bull,
And the fox leapt up and the tentacle missed narrowly,
And the fox fell to the ground,
Breaking a leg.
The sheep, laughing a horrible shrill,
Circled the air, and spiraled down to the fox,
Who was limping towards the ladder.
The ladder disintegrated into dust and ashes,
And the fox was covered in it.
The sheep touched down, and grabbed the fox by the throat,
With its gorilla hands, saying,

"The fox should have stayed in his world.
Now the fox will become one with my world,
One with the ground and the dirt!"
And sheep squeezed hard,
And the fox began to cry,
And yelp for help.
The sheep grinned and was about to
Make his death squeeze,
Until its ears detected a
Snap of a twig.

The sheep turned, the fox still dangling in its hands,
The corpse of the monster was charging,
Limping and bleeding and stomping,
And a great force filled the air,
And as it opened its mouth,
Broken and unsymmetrical it was,
The sheep turned to parry, releasing the fox,
But it was too late.
The monster had gained the
Advantage of surprise,
And with its Trusty Whip
The monster strangled the sheep,
Until its eleven foot neck
No longer moved.
Ripping the body to seven pieces,
The monster rested.

The fox asked the monster how it was still alive,
And no reply came.
Its heaving head did not turn.
The fox nodded, and looked towards the sky.

A chariot rode by,
And on the back of the chariot
Was a man, with a baseball cap on.
He held out his hand,
And with one last look,
The fox leapt up,
And looked at the monster
And he flew away with the kind stranger.
The monster didn't move,
But only became smaller and smaller
As they flew higher into the clouds.

The fox asked the man,
"Where are we going? Where are you taking me?"

And the human smiled,
And they flew on, ahead of them anything and
everything.

LUCID TRANSPARENCY

Where the meadow ends,
Transform!
Where the rainbow begins,
Multiply!
Be your own African famine
And depopulate your heart
Son of Adam.

SAVANNAH LOVE CHILD

Pleasurable fancies of a time so far ago,
Frills and tea, powdered wigs and stickball,
Where is my mother?
Freshen your mouth with minty recollection,
Layered upon cinnamon flavored love.
The taste is too bitter for an animal
But for humans it is divine.

Peace be to you, Lion-Brother.
You growl at the hyena and you do not dance.
If you get an email,
You would eat the computer,
And not know why you died.
Scientists would tell me electrolysis,
And I would laugh in their face,
And then eat them, in memory of you.

When will I die?
When science is dead.
Until then, I eat on.

UNIFICATION OF FORM

Fountain, fountain,
Give me light.
Take me away from Earth,
Passport to the stars
Trickle down,
And set me to freedom!

BILATERAL HUSBANDRY

Dog walking vixen,
Set your terrier on me,
And we will fight in glory.
Come round again,
Your dog is more appealing to me
Than your hideous face.
You turn in vanity,
And smirk in ignorance,
Where will you be when the job market comes?

ADDICTION

Coffee bean, coffee bean,
You enslaving master.
Enter my realm and energize my parts!
I trust you with my day,
Do not fail me:
I'm running a marathon.

DOOR SWINGIN' MORTALITY

Whistle from your horse
Rugged cowboy.
Your whistle is just a mask
For your idiocy.
Do you know where the trail leads?
Of course not.
Give up and lasso yourself.

LIFE LESSONS

Lonely fat man, get a job.
You sit for hours, waiting for a
Macaroni that will
Burn away while you sleep.

APPREHEND THE THIEF

You who cut my hair
Be warned.
I have snakes on my scalp
That will tear you apart.
Wash with caution and anti-snake lotion!

You who pump my gas
Listen close.
I keep lions in my tank:
Hungry ones.
They will tackle you.

You who court me,
Final warning.
The Roman Gladiator Secret Service (RGSS)
I keep in my front pocket.
They will slice your head off, secretly,
In front of screaming fans.

Do not toy with my heart,
For I am a bellowing beast machine.

FREEWAY APARTMENT

Noisy lights of green!
I cannot sleep!
Where is my gun?

PEACE AND LOVE

37 to 39 cents?
Mail is the Devil.
My throat hurts.

AN ALIEN'S CHOICE

Robot parts would rust,
Spoons would get old,
Swords would prohibit job opportunity,
Spaghetti would rot,
Cinder blocks too heavy
Plants ineffective,
Water improbable
And chains not useful.
I will keep my arms, thank you.

SUBDUED AND MISTAKEN PHILOSOPHY

Seagulls annoy me
Sewage disgusts me
Sand itches me
Water wets me
And somehow I love the beach,
But hate daytime television.

ITALY

Red is the color of my love
Green is the color of my train
White is the color of my skin
I wear boots.

CIRCUS O LAY

Round and round we go
A merry go round made of candy
Eat and fall off, starve and ride!
What do you choose?
Throwing up was not an option!
Now we are riding a sticky, gross
Candy merry go round,
And I hate you.

PREDICTION

Look at us, we're so great
We're tall and thin,
Rich and cool,
And on a date!
Stroll around with arms all locked,
Laughing saying funny things
We dance and drink
And go to clubs
And in our car we kiss.
And everything it goes so well
We have no problems
None at all!

We're made for each other
Look at us
We're attractive!
Let's have sex!
Then the fairy tale ended and
Three weeks later we both
Hated each other and ended
Up with STDs.
We're broke and
What were we thinking?

Just kidding, we're so great!
Hug me, love me, more more more
Let's do this again!
Is there any meaning to all this?
Oh no! A tornado!

PREDICTION PART II

I'll calm down with you, honey.
Let's go for a walk tonight.
Shirk our cares
We'll be cold together
As we walk in the wind.
I love you, truly.
I do, too.
Hold my hand, and let's just
Be.

Oh no! A tornado!

MARS CRAZY

Help me to dig this hole!
I want to dig something!
Shovel, throw, repeat!
What are you doing?
You are crazy!
You can't throw, repeat, shovel!
You deserve what you get.
Back to the hospital with you.

FUN IN THE SUN

Worked all day today.
The night is here.
Concubine! Feed me grapes!
Are we not happy, concubine?
Dance the dance of grapes, concubine!
Fool!
That is the dance of melons!
Clod!
Be gone from my sight,
And bring me my jester!
What? It is morning?
Fine. I go back to work.
Tonight you dance appropriately!

LOGIC

The higher you go,
The better you are.
If that's true,
Men who drive lifted trucks
Should bow
Before the Sherpas of the Himalayas.

AFTERPARTY

It is a manner of principle.
Up is down, and down is not.
Make no sense and you shall
I grow tired of fame
Who wants bananas?

ARROW

I wish to put my mind on a shelf,
And sell it to the angels,
Who will throw it high in
The sky,
And it will float without gravity
Never landing, but always traveling,
But my earthly body will be dead.

FEARFUL

Why not find a cure for all diseases?
I will tell you:
Because of pillows.
The super healthy don't need rest
And there goes the pillow business.
It's a conspiracy
Of pillow executives
Who themselves don't sleep
But make money and
Are super-bots.

FIT

You are my beauty in a jar
That I cannot open
Or break into.

VISION

A spiral slide down a steep hill.

MIRACLE

Eclectic women dance in the night
Round a moon on the ground
Sacrifices to the blessed crow,
A ceremony for the ageless
"Drab and shnook
and toof nib boon"
And now there's no such thing as bees.

WATCHDOG

A hill.
You.
A tree.
Shadow.
Sunset.
Stream.
Golden.
Warm.
Walking.
Reeds.

Closer.
Bigger.
Closer.
You.
Touch.
Hold.
Kiss.
Moment.
Eyes.
Heart.
Tornado!

YOU ARE MIDDLE AMERICAN

A lesson learned is wisdom gained.
The honey jar bites.
A lesson learned is wisdom gained.
The honey jar bites!
A lesson learned is wisdom gained.
Hey, this honey jar bites!
A lesson learned is wisdom gained.
Ow! Does anyone know this honey jar bites?
A lesson learned is wisdom gained.
My hand is gone!
A lesson learned is wisdom gained.
The honey jar bit my hand off!
A lesson learned is wisdom gained.
What kind of honey jar is this?
A lesson learned is wisdom gained.
I'm going to put my face in it…
A lesson learned is wisdom gained.
It bit my head off!

HUNTER GATHERER

The bump of rhythm hollows the room
My soul is fulfilled
Free flowing lyrics breathe
Heavily on me
Down with the solstice!
Rap never changed the hour
Of the day
Or shortened the sunlight.
Burn your skin on a pan
And feel the pain of a long shadow
On an expectant morn!
Command legions and know not
The responsibility of my gravity.
Feathers and pilgrims
Unite
To find
A common ground,
On which both can fly
And both are rocky.
Boxing is changed forever!
Pilots have front row
Seats
For the 'fly flight' debut.
A Cave I save for you, my love.

AGELESS TIME WARP

Shadow on the wall
Train at the port
Man on the moon
Fruit on the fly
Sickle on the flag
Me with the sky
You in my head,
Soon we'll all be dead.

LOW–CUT TOP

Vibrant sounds on conversation
A trickle and a tickle from a stranger
Pierce the navel of your enemy
And become an idolater of faiths.
Matter-horn beams
A translucent light
Onto an oblong face.
And out of the shadows,
Fairies pay a homage
To a
Fallen leader
When is time stopping?
Does anyone know how to stop
A fairy army?

HEMISPHERE

An ideal of the mind,
A look of the eyes,
The two are cousins!
Marry the two, you incestuous scientist!
Bubble your beakers,
Trouble your tweakers
And mix the love of blood
For an ideal look
Looks ideal
At a wedding.

HOMECOMING

Bitter honey will soften
The noblest soldier
In an apple blossom raid.
Imagine the wood splints
Necessary to promulgate a species
Until it is frozen in sexual heat.

UNTITLED

A familiar face rings true
And lies always buzz flase
The wet pavement is no place
For an eel such as yourself
You may feel at home here
Because it is water-like,
But I am human!
I will drive my car over

Your tail
And you will scream
In an unknown, slithering language
That not even the sewer rats
Will understand.
Back to the refuse with you
You scale-less slime of the
Earth!
None will miss you!
I throw you to the street!

What is that in your mouth?
My self confidence?
What do you do with my self confidence?
Give it back
Wretched scum!
No, do not bite down
Slime of slime and slimes!
My self confidence bleeds!
It is tender, medium rare, and mine
If I don't get it back,
I'll end up like that guy,
Making not funny remarks
All day
To a barista who doesn't care.

BLUE COFFEE

A first meeting
Talk about your relatives
Your electronics
Your job

Your personality
Display your wit
Your attraction
Your confidence
Your wealth
Hide your nervousness
Your fears
Your doubts
Your self absorption
Drink your coffee
Crack your jokes
Widen your smile
Feign your interest
Flip your hair
Nod your head
Shift your body
Wink your eye

Make your move
Soon it will all be over
The decision will be made
And you will be left
Waving on a street corner
To someone
You may never see again
So go hard and strong
And set your hook
And do what you can
To get them back
They've already made a
Decision

And as you say goodbye
Look as though you
Are kissing them
And piercing their heart.
Make the last image of you,
You alone.
For all week
It is only you.

BAROQUE GET ME DOWN

Saxophone grease pours on
Your belly,
The jazz of our love!
Trumpet juice spews on
Your face!
The jazz of our love!
Drum kits bang and explode
On your head!
The jazz of our love!
You're not moving.
Why?
Do you not like the jazz of our love?
Or are you dead?

NONE OF THE ABOVE

An infernal sound
Is the wind in the morning.
Think you can withstand the toil?
Stand on a trail
Mega-listeners on each ear,

Three in all.
And wait for Fate to
Beckon the horse wind to reign.
Then, and only then,
Will
The door open.

TIME

Can babes understand?
Here is the test.
If a sound is made
When a bowling ball is dropped
You will know what they know.
For if a bowling ball falls
And water is loose
Than can young ever be young again?

PEACE IN A RIFF

Is it neat to fit in?
Do you scratch your scalp for
Acceptance?
Wash away your tears,
Joaquin,
With my suburban washcloth.
A line of Congressmen
Awaits
To shake your hand,
And they've all
Paid
A pretty penny.
Joaquin, you sun-god!

MARGARET

What's a staaaamp?

ST. PETER

I thought the streets were
Made of gold,
Until closer I looked,
And got mustard on my nose.

ROYAL MIGS

Three mustaches do I see:
A bald man looks left out.
But all four smiling the same
I wish I had a feather
In my cap
To knight
The brave man
Who stands
Among
Proud and laughing
And smiles all the same
Though the same he may not be.
A party!

EXPEDITE THE SEWAGE

Reach for a pig,
Get a horse
Reach for money,

Get a punch in the face
Reach for a girl
And get depression
Why are they all like a dirty pair of jeans
In the clean clothes drawer?
Is it possible to wash them?

O. T.

The end bears such a sad tone
If only we had salmon
Tim would bid thee farewell,
For a price, of course, for he is greedy,
A fine meal exerts great energy
And the Sutton demands respect!
No longer do I mourn the dead!
Their fate is angrier than I!
And I envy them!
Grave robbing would be a noble deed,
For heirlooms of kings have ye!
The rulers of Earth hide the truth
And it is in the ground!
Wash your fruit!
Crazy girl.
You unbound sojourner
Come back here and pity me
I wish to play a piano on you
Live the deeds of Hercules
Half god, half goat-man
You fiend!
And when the time comes
To swan or swane

Only a hero will
Swan
And a pathetic wretch will swane
The flow of emotion
Belies
Men themselves
But no match
For the now.

PUMPKIN PIE

A ripped napkin that scars the heart
With a green cap to cap in your thoughts.
Black thoughts will die!
The sun will smile!
In a womb of mercy
You will cirsumvrent the law!
Daughter of Destruction,
I beg you to release
The dog
That protects
My lungs
From you.

ENGAGEMENT

Melancholy music softens your ears,
And a young potential mate
Sets my eyes afire
I drink away my tears
And come back to the safari,
For I'm not allowed
To take my love

Back with me
On the plane.
But I forever dream…

GRIDLOCK

The hyena awaits
The next generation
And a star studded
Loophole
Diseases the contract
Between nature
And skyscraper.

LYNCH–MOB–GROWL

Yours and mine
Together they lie
Somewhere on a financial chart
Run your finger
Up the line
And see our house,
Our kids,
Our dog,
Part of a prediction
Prophesized by some figure
Whose face is a dollar symbol
And whose pen
Is the ink of money.
Rebel from the line!
Find your white picket fence!
The dog that barks there
Is twice in the same spot
A dimension awaits you and your pride.

RETURN TO VALVELAND

The deal:
Drink this flagon,
And greens will be purple.
Swallow this pill,
And businessmen will be
Giant paper bags.
Sign on this line,
And windows will chase you down.
Can you deal
Deal you I?
Think not of preliminary theories.
Because all we need is
To hold my hand
And the deal is sealed.

INHALE STAPLES

Car parts are intricate
And so is sex.
And if I can't start the engine,
It's no fault of mine,
Because I am six,
And my bike has no ignition.

FINAL COURTSHIP

Blender,
Blend your 'great girl' mix,
The shake you make
Is putrid to all.

A shadow on me
Tells of a presence
Of corporate jokes
And I awkwardly throw up
On a board meeting
And now I am on pulse
And liquefy is not an option
As I make my speech.

MANE LINE

Fascinating what bears will do.
I am a lion.
I know nothing of bear affairs.
Except that
What the hell is that bear
Doing in the Sahara?
I am a learned lion,
Who knows his geography.

RIGHT QUESTION

A groove in the rain forest,
Is still a groove,
Except that it is wet
And endangered.

QUICK FOX, RUN!

The look of a female
Causes me to tremble.
But a bullet
Only kills me.

TWEED AND SHERRY

Slide into place
Until it locks
And burns your tongue
And violence
Is the meaning
Of the fruit
That bears the name.

WALK IN AND SING

Green clock,
Circle round,
Down and out,
Brown hair,
Wooden chair,
Another commercial,
Easy beat,
Fast and slow snaps,
Trash on the sill,
Ear music,
Over coat,
Windy city,
Jazz kitchen,
Peace and appearance,
And a man I've
Never met before
Speaks in a language
That's familiar,
But speaks only
To one—
Silence.

TIME TO GO

The bread you find
Is green
But the water man is back.
What flirtatious
Offering
Will we have
For this princess?
I see a white shirt
And a loose neck.
Your head will fall
Off from
The shock
Of an empty proposal.
I need a paper clip
To warn the people
About your treachery.

WINDY

A firm grip on the armament
Secures justice.
Plague and villain
Combine into an awful
Repugnance.
Advertisements harden
A fierce force of down feathers
And ants crawl
From a screaming homeless man.

MESOPOTAMIA

The flavor of the wind
Is cherry,
But an apple blossom will
Rise with its sword
And slay the farmer
Who penetrated its life
For a profit
Of clam shells
The barter system is over!

DOUBLE BACK FLIP

The lonely orange tree
Sways and sways
And thinks all is well
The busy ant is up the hill
And he, too,
Thinks all is well.
The little sheep,
Ice skating and doing a triple lutz,
Thinks all is well.

From up on high Zeus is angry,
No longer will
Trees sway,
Ants crawl,
Or sheeps skate.
A terrible flood
And a heavy cannonball
Fall from the kingly clouds.

The anthill is flooded,
The sheep is crushed,
But the lonely orange tree
Still sways and sways.

QUIET YOU

My thumb has seen
Amazing places.

ICED TEA

Don't shake your head.
That just means you're sad.
And what do we do with sad people?
That's right.
And you can't swim.
Or withstand a barrage of bullets
So smile!

DETERGENT DAY

The train comes, I await it
At the station.
A chug-a-lug-chug. A chug-a-lug-chug.
I can see it far away,
It makes a strange noise.
A chug-a-lug-chug. A chug-a-lug-chug.
My suitcase is at my feet,
Packed with firecrackers
A chug-a-lug-chug. A chug-a-lug-chug.
Faster, faster, goes the train

My vacation has almost begun.
A chug-a-lug-chug. A chug-a-lug-chug.
Sunny beaches and cynical women
Await me.

Blackness.

I missed my train.
I chug-a-lug-chugged too much beer
At the station
And passed out.
Oh well. Back to work.

ACHE

All glitz and glamour's
My life is everything.
I always get what I want
There's always friends around me,
My favorite food is aged ham,
Melted muenster cheese,
And eggs of a whale.
I will never die
I am a wonder!
Bow down!
I come to your town!
But if you wish to dine me,
And wine me,
Do not serve lobster,
For I am allergic.

JOINT AT THE NIP

A man in a brown sweater walks,
Walk down the street and smile in the heat,
Heat a pot of tea, will you?
You love me, or else I will go away
Away with you, Jester! I tire of your jokes.
Joke not of my fat, I am sensitive
Sensitivity is much wanted among women
Women are bear traps that mostly are nice
Nice weather and bees go together
Together we walk down the aisle
Aisle six has cheese
Cheese is made from the milk of a cow
Cow meat is prohibited in these parts
Part man, part machine!
Machines do more harm than good
Good job, pelican. You fished well.
Well, well, well. Mr. Tumnus.
Tumnus is my uncle. I am fierce
Fierce is the revenge of a twin brother.
Brother. Hermano. Brothero!

LOGICAL ECONOMY

A cackling laugh in the distance
Is she crazy?
Am I attracted to her?
She wears a dress of gears
And cranks into place
And rises up a hundred yards
And stretches her bulky arms

And lifts her head to the sky
And takes a bite out of the sun
And roars with delight
And uses cars as crumbs
And thrusts her hands
Through the Chrysler building
And gold is valuable!

WHAT IS JACK?

One step further,
And I drop your cousin
Into the acid tank.
Give me the blueprints!

ROCKHOUND

The year is 1985
And that's all you need to know.

BEFITTING FOR KNIGHT

Turn your head slightly to the left
And give me
Your best
Marlon Brando impersonation.
Then cough.

Okay, you're fine.

APPEAL–SEX STYLE

One o'clock strikes
And the easy fate queens
Are nowhere to be seen.
There will be
No rumble today.

GAME SIMPLE

The long hair of Samson
Is easy to cut.
All you need are Delilah's
Looks,
Sex appeal,
Deceptiveness,
Stealth,
Corruptibility,
And scissors.

HOME LESSONS

It's too easy to be cold.
What's hard
Is to have class.

DIS

If you have a door
Held open for you
And you don't even
Look me in the eye,

Much less say thank you,
The next time I see you
I will trip you
And pour applesauce
Down your pants, and say
Have a nice day,
Applesauce pants.

SO SHE KNOWS

Caution!
There is a time ahead
When permontion
Bounces up and down
Like a daddy's little
Claus
And a warning forgoes
All knowledge.
Merry Christmas!

PROP 38

In this bag
Are the secrets of the world,
And I will sell them to you
For one dollar.

GUESSING GAME

Like an apple,
I bear leaves,
But more like a pear,
I can pounce, growl, snarl,
Tear, leap, bound, see, hear,
Taste, touch, smell, drink,
Eat, wipe, run,
Bid on stock,
Write memos,
And press buttons.

GOOD MORNING TOKYO

Fingers roll up and down
Tap your feet
Bounce and bounce
And halt.
And go–
And rhythm fast in your soul
And the feel of a twist
Round and back
And just the bass
Drums around
Is that a pick?
Groove…
Is the rhythm
Piano man
Play a little faster
Everyone now
One at a time
Crescendo out.

BEAM AGE

The one who saw you fall
The man who witnessed you throw up
The woman who rejected you
The postman who laughed at you
When you tried to mail a napkin,
The teacher who questioned you,
When you turned in a paper entitled,
"Why the Greeks Rocked,"
The technician who couldn't believe
You didn't know where the power switch was
The dog who growled at you
The cat that gave you fleas
The driver who would almost run you over
The talk show host that annoyed you
Will all most likely
Be dead before you.
So go have an ice cream cone
And celebrate.

B–RIGHT BACK

The little man with a cap on
Rolls thorugh the streets
As though they are his.
With passion and vigor
He struts the slippery,
Snow-covered sidewalks,
And scowls at those around him.
Who are they to look at him,
The owner of this town?
He slips on the ground,
And everyone knows.

CYCLE

83 is a giant
that will soon be 84
that was once 82
And where does the time go?

SWEATY PALMS

My bones called me today
And told me
To start drinking more milk.
My mind called me today
And asked me
To read more books.
My feet called me today
And told me
To stop taking the stairs.
My ex-girlfriend called me today
And warned me
To stop sending her flowers at work, or she's calling the
cops.
My legs called me today
And told me
To wear pants on cold days
My self esteem called me today
And told me
To stop whining and shut the hell up
My dad called me today
And was concerned:
The cops were looking for me.
The florist called me today

To confirm
Did I say 10,000 roses to that address? Yes.
A bum called me today
To thank me for the donut I gave him.
(How he got a phone, I don't know.)
My psychologist called me today
I think it was a prank call.
My lawyer called me today
To say
There's nothing more he can do.
My friends called me today
To wish me good luck
In my incarceration.

How am I going to live
With only one phone call?

READ AND RIGHT

Sitting on the edge of time,
Breaking the limits of understanding
Bits and pieces o' fun
In broken glass houses.
The windy city blows lines
Of fury,
A cold, commented breeze
That spits out
A scraped, grass-stained knee.

EMOLUTION

Another rampage
Stilled by a blinking sonar.
Another court jester
Thrown aside by kings of philanthropy
Another decade
Embezzled by disgruntled bananas.
These are the times
In which man eats man
For the purpose of survival.
Survival of the wittiest!

SALUTATIONS

Orange juice
Banana
Coffee
Bread
If I took a hundred of these
At once
I'd be dead.

CARBOHYDRATES

A man and his face are soon parted
With my man-and-face splitting machine.

IN THE NAME OF YOUR FATHER

Ice clinks in the mouth grinder,
An action star flashes a badge.
A winking eye tells all
And sets things in motion
A ripped paper
A broken contract
A tattered heart
An exploding prison cell
The will to live
The incessant rain
An empty vending machine
Damn it!
A dropped coffee mug
A hurried walk
An open window
A phony salute
A smile
A scream
A run
The jump
The fall
The death
The brushing of soldiers
The walk away.

MICKLE- TICKLE

I've discovered a thing
Better than being wasted.
Just stick your head in a deep fryer
And hold it there

Until your hair is crispy.
When you come out,
You'll have a French fry head,
And will have
At least
Two full meals
Before you eat your whole head
And die.

ARE Y.A.O.T.D.

The two silhouettes are talking
To each other.
What do they say?
They exert no sound
And yet say all.
Poised on chairs of power,
They indeed shake hands
For other reasons.
Run with them,
They are yours.
Be proud of their money.
Yet do not reach for them.
A dark future awaits these
Who touch the silhouettes.
One day it may be
A three handed shake
And you will look out of place.

DAY #2

A calming wind
Loves the shadow of a tree.
And as I sit here
Feeling them both,
I cannot help but think
About how wet my pants are.
Why is this grass so wet?

SMOKEY CLAV

Boots up to your thighs,
A skirt of a single rubber band,
A top of nothing
And a paper bag over your face.
You have never been
Less appealing!

HOLE IN THE WALL

You cannot buy me a bracelet,
Because I have no wrists!

THE HACKEY CLUB

A young maiden
With bright red hair
Tilts her face sideways.
She is peculiar,
Interesting,
Unpredictable.
It makes me sad to see her

Walking into that gorge.
I'd yell to warn her,
But my throat hurts,
And it's too far to hear, anyway.

A TALE OF CITYHOOD

The trumpets intimate a glorious arrival,
Promises of fruits and spices abound.
The village whispers of heroic tales,
And the glorious hero who will return.
For days he has been anticipated,
And has finally arrived!
The day has come,
Preparations made,
The palm leaves are laid out
He and his mighty army are heard
From little child to big cat.
Confetti is held in the hands of the excited
And balloons are ready for release
Green! Red! Blue! The colors!
They wait on the rooftops for the supreme moment
When rumor will meet reality
As a clicking puzzle piece.

And then the moment comes.
The sound of feet marching
The city is ready
All breath is held
Gasp!
Gasp!
Eyes widen!
The voices scream!

At the front of the army
Leading the masses,
Is an empty peanut shell.
Tall as a man, moving as one, too,
He (or it) hobbles down the road.

This is not our hero!
Expectant faces are puzzled and confused
"Do we cheer for the peanut shell?"
"Where is our masculine leader?"
"Where is his armor?"
"Where is his sword?"
"Where is his face?"
No answers given by none
The peanut shell leads on,
Confetti still held,
Balloons ready, not moving,
The decision is halted,
For the peanut shell has stopped.
Tilting its body back, it surveys as a man would.
And just like a man, it is given attention.
A pause of utter silence from the masses.
Can it talk?

A little child believes it can and yells
"Speech! Speech!"
A larger child catches on and yells
"Speech! Speech!"
A young man, an older man, everyone else:
"Speech! Speech!"
The peanut shell jumps up and down

And regains its attention.
Surely if this is our hero he will tell us so,
And we will believe him.
At the moment where a speech was expected,
The peanut shell cracked in two,
Falling to the ground in pieces.

Awe and hush,
Hush and awe.

Pandemonium in the streets!
Riots on the rooftops!
Fire, breaking, bashing, burning!
Yelling, hitting, looting, screaming!
Chaos, confusion, and pain!
Chaos, confusion, and pain!

Where is our leader?
We expected him to come, and he did not!
We expected a hero, and all we got
Was an empty peanut shell!
There is no hope for us!
Pillage your neighbor! Leaders are dead!

The town killed itself.
The army watched it all. Calm. Collected.
They watched the bell tower fall.
They watched the church burn.
They watched the preschool crumble.
They watched it all.

Out of the ordered lines came a young girl
After days of pillaging, she had seen enough.
She raised her palm to the sky,
Flat and powerful.
The army stood at attention.
She cleared her throat, and
With a loud boom, she bellowed
Two words.
Let it be known that these words
Pierced the hearts of all in the town
And the survivors, upon hearing the words,
Changed forever.
With her golden hair flowing in the wind,
She cried out the words.

And with that, the town was changed.
No longer did they need a leader.
No more confetti
No more balloons
No more admiration for no one.

And in their hearts each of the survivors
Killed the golden haired little girl
She lived on in obscurity
Never to be thought of by the town again
She would return with her army
A veces,
But the town would close its gates,
She no longer held power there.

And the town lived on. In peace.
And the town lived on.

CULTURE

It's easy to see morals
In a mirror of saints.
But hark!
Mushy, muddy Bibles
Reveal a symptom of parallelograms
That inflicts the roots
Of every tribesman
Gossiping about the newest
Hallucinogen.
Is that a parrot?

AVAILABILITY OF SPIRIT

Snow rumbles and tumbles,
And the beat goes on.
Our journey is halted,
And the rats above laugh
And throw tomatoes,
But the beat goes on.
Echoes from a past
Of sin
Reverberate
Like Bach's 2nd symphony,
And his passion redeems it,
While the beat goes on.
The hands get dirtier
While climbing,
But an author's only
Gets inky,
And can do both.

ZINGER

A rush of what to the head?
I don't believe in that.

KNPASACK DIARIES

The fan swings round the room
And can't find it's bearing
Until the light switches on.
Now the room is cool and lit well.

PISS POOR

Circles are everywhere
Except in Squaresville.
In Squaresville there are only squares,
The circles can only see it
From a distance.
And when the circles try to get in,
They are shot down by square guards
On the high walls.
And no one weeps for the circles,
Except the circles, (and a few ovals,
Who are far away but do nothing.)
I took an eraser and erased the dead cicrles,
And wished I could do the same to
Everyone else.
Instead,
The squares darken themselves
With a felt pen,
And then publish themselves
In the New Yorker.

FEAST OF AGES

Fruit is a reward
For toil in the soil.
I use it for a pillow!
Cherries dot my dreams,
And blueberries are my blanket!
The toil is all around me,
And I am the reward!
Avocados try to warm my feet,
And I kick them
And dip my chips in the result.

MIDDLE OF SIGHT

Rescue me, brave fireman.
Lift me from my burning place
And fly me away to a pool.
The fire grows hot
Where are you?
I need coffee, please.
What are you doing here?
I'm waiting for a fireman.
Where did this couch come from?
The street is empty, save for the couch.
Your dress is flowery
My father doesn't like you
And neither do my friends
Right field? In front of everyone?
Why am I checking IDs?
Basketball!
Ah!
Breathing hard. Lie down.

INTE-SEXUAL

Deliver me no more water.
I am no longer thirsty.
Medea is plotting, and I need
A Deus Ex Machina.
A fountain of youth!
Can you give me that water?
Midas was wrong!

THE TALE OF A BEING ONCE REMOVED

I once walked across a desert
For three days.
This is my account.

It's a story
Of adventure,
Love,
Betrayal, sacrifice,
And self-discovery.
At the end,
Please applaud, if you
Feel the need to.

Upon a morn of distant yore,
Received I a message from a distant land.
A loved one of long ago
Was in a peril that she could not overcome.
She pleaded for my arrival,
Begging for my *ayuda*,

And though she had lain with another
During the spring of our love,
Her necessity was greater than my anger.
So in my obliged state I
Walked onto my porch,
And desert was all around me.
Some men say to live
In nature is the greatest deed.
I live in the desert,
Alone and separate from all.
In the morning I watch the sun
Rise over the mesas far,
And sip a coffee, brewed fresh and strong.
The solitary life is the life
For me.
Although it is a full days walk for groceries.
So I buy in bulk.

Upon that day I left to help
My former love,
I thought that I might stop
At Old Man Gilley's for a cantaloupe.
It was on the way.
With a gallon of water,
A pound of rice, a tent, a hat,
Sunscreen, sunglasses, sand shoes,
And Dixie cups, I started.
Old Man Gilley's was a day away:
A walk I was used to.

The usual things occurred
That first day.
Exhaustion, sweating, singing, etc.
But one thing stands out in my mind:
When I was attacked by a vulture.

Swooping down from the heavens above,
His great wings fluttering like
Hundreds of moths.
With my sonic super ears
I heard his cry, and turned
As it swept by,
Missing my face with its
Eagle fang claws.
I crouched again as it came around
Again.
Wait for it…
Wait for it…
Now!
As it cawed and screamed and lunged forward,
I threw myself backwards and onto the ground,
And took out my sword and
Swung upwards,
Slashing
In a semi-circle above my head.
The bright sun was shaded
By the body for only a moment
Before that shade was split in two.

The dust settled, and I wiped my eyes,
Standing, there were two halves
Of the shadow on either side of me.

A spot of black on my nose
I wipe off with a sandy hand.
Tattered and victorious,
I am a soldier.
Holding up the head of my enemy in one hand,
I stab the air with my sword in the other,
And scream to the vast emptiness,
"I am weather!"
And there is silence
In the desert for a time.

Until

Caw.
Turn my head.
Caw caw.
Turn the other way.
Caw! Caw! Caw!
Search the sky.
And in an instant,
As flies scurry to a pile
Of dung,
A swarm of vultures
Advances towards me,
A black cloud of death,
Closer and closer they caw.
With incessant screeches.

Apparently their leader
I took.
Without hesitation I run
Toward the pack of cawing devils.

I heave myself
And as the first line of winged
Avengers
Approach,
I   jump.
Scream.
Grab hold.
Before I know it I am
Riding an enemy.
It screams and caws and dips
To get me off,
But my hold is firm,
Its feathers crunching in my white fist,
As the others around me peck and dive,
I slash them to the ground
To the left- slash!
To the right- slash!
They fall far, and looking down
Is a chore.
We tour the sky and the clouds
Together
I with my ride
I with my mirth
I with my strength
And vulture with the ground
And vulture with the ground.
Hundreds upon hundreds
Of fallen heads, wings, feather.
And as the sky is clear all
Around me
(except for the friend beneath me)
I knew I had all but won.

The misty cloud in my face,
I plunged my sword into the neck of my foe
Who gave me flight.
We both fell down together,
Like two rocks,
Spinning out of control.
Reaching for its wings I positioned
Myself underneath,
Stretching out to grab both wings.
Sword in my teeth,
I started flapping,
My might was my strength,
And before we could hit the ground,
We were flying,
Touching down gently.
I threw the villain
Off my back
And spit in his dead face.
The giant yellow sun fell
Beneath the hill,
And the carcasses
Made a good tent
As the desert cold wrapped around me.

Day the second proved to be
An illustrious day indeed!
The morn greeted me with sandy
Winds that turned me round,
So all direction was lost.
Wandering like a babe set free
In the nursery,
I was dry throated and tired.

And in the distance I saw
Old man Gilley
Shrouded in an Arabian blanket
That was given as a gift three years previous.
I walked into the saloon styled
Merchant store.
Old Man Gilley was crazy with power.
He popped balloons in my face
On purpose!
And cackled in the dark
As he threw pointed arrows at my legs.
So I sat in the saloon and talked
With my old friend,
Telling him of my journey and intents.
He told me his pride flowed hard
And wanted to help me.
But first he would tell me a story
Of his own.
Though I was parched with thirst,
I obliged him to go on.
Turning down the lights,
Like a perverted sunset,
He lit a cigarette and puffed his story
Towards me, and said,
"I a young lad like you once,"
(the old, crazy man was plagued
not only
with smallpox,
but with oratory dyslexia.)

"And day flower girl liked I one she and
beautiful tower sat saw a a minefield.

Said came and why me she to at if with do
You as a stare I me were slave lobsters?
You I girl and are have the said most most
World in beautiful I you.
And guard is me the that you must
To field it that no matter very I cross,
I the side that would like, time to get
Other by I that the you I married and
Looked blue took at she me so her Nazi it
And at eyes out me and with Beretta pointed,
One step down 'I put like you won't you
Take the saying, more' and dog hesitate to resemble,
With moving Gable, she and and like to hard
I trembled and kept and wept smile forward Clark her,
Out gun it and I gently love-struck down to her
Reached her my and get hand touched helped it
Demeanor resist and to she started my young she
Couldn't and me bucking and relented cry,
And we kissed.
But a she as stepped first and steps blew
Couple we new took wrong our she as up.
I've never loved since."

I was about ready to
Hit the man for his nonsense
But he stopped.
"Lodging do I need,
more than abject stories of uneducated
swallows."
With a biting glare he agreed
That the candle wax was low
And so to bed we must go.

He arose first in the morning.
Shaking the bed as he got up.
When I awoke fully
He was gone
As was the house!
I awoke with dust in my
Mouth,
The sun beating down as an elf does,
My compass spoke
And told of the exact location
Of where we had slept.
Was it all a dream?
No need to dwell
On the reality of the dwelling.

Day the third had begun.
One more day
Nightfall would bring me my former love.
As feet shuffled and lips licked dry,
Mind wandered afar…
To why I was there.
The trip had been long
And hard
And for what?
Why do I sacrifice
For a love no longer felt?
Conclusions came not so easily,
And soon a light came I
Could not accept,
And put it away as foolishness.

Pass the Route A13,
Across the dune of Dukeman,
Over the cactus fields of
Sir Amud de le Torre.
A sound in the distance.
Crowd. Applause. Cheers.
A coliseum? In the desert?
It was true.
And on the board of events
What did I see
But the name of my love
In letter bigger than clouds,
And next to hers, the name
"Vs. The Dragon."

I ran and ran to the stadium,
Where Romans and Greeks alike
Were paying shekels to get
A furlong farther to watch the
Games that were a tribute to
Leif Erikson.
Pushed I did through togas, sandals,
Sunglasses, floaties, deceptions, and dogs.
Into a clearing in the stands.
I surveyed the arena.

Two hundred thousand cheering fans,
Attentions all on the center arena,
Dusty and hard.
The pre-show attraction was pleasing
To all.
An elephant on its hind legs,

Balancing fourteen chairs on its upturned trunk,
And atop the highest chair,
Sat a whiskered fellow,
Juggling hunks of meat,
Breathing fire,
And cooking the meat as it passed
Through the flame.
And all the while, on the ground,
Surrounding the elephant,
Hundreds of high school band members
Did a choreographed dance.
The conductor was a bear
In a bell hop's outfit,
His conducting wand a canary,
That kept trying to escape.
At the conclusion of the song
The elephant did a full
Front flip on a giant trampoline,
The chairs and whiskered man
Stayed with it,
But one hunk of meat flew out
Of control
And plugged a tuba,
And the child playing it
Blew too hard
And his face became red and exploded,
At which the crowd cheered.
This was the end of the pre-show.

I searched the crowd, and found
Erikson.
In a rich man's box, halfway up the

Stadium,
He sat on an ivory throne,
Eating live turtles that crunched
Over the loud speakers.
He spoke perfect Spanish through
The turtle crunches,
And gave his blessing to the performers,
Telling the audience to
Take their seventh inning stretch
While the arena was cleared
For the main event.
He also said to use the bathroom,
Only if you must,
The act would be coming soon.

I needed to hurry.
Clearly my love needed saving
From "Vs. The Dragon,"
Whoever that was.

Then I saw her.

A gate opened at one end of
The oval arena,
A majestic gate
That the elephant and his chairs
Barely fit through on their way out.
She came out, chained to a
Flagpole on a platform with wheels.
The flag I did not recognize,
But it was nevertheless lit afire
By a flaming arrow from the crowd.

Most objected, but when they
Turned to see who it was
Who shot it,
All were quiet,
For Socrates demands respect,
And he stood there, nodding to Erikson,
Who looked away.
The fire was left burning
As the platform was pushed out
By trolls.

The visage of her face
Flashed me back a thousand years
To when we first met.

'Twas the night before Christmas
and I, a sad and lonely
fellow of chivalry
had given up my seat
at a local parlor to a lady
who in turn spilled her café on me.
Lonesome was I, and
Took I a walk through the
Night time promenade.
An apple occupied my mouth
And the bittersweet chewing
And cold air
And hustle and bustle
Made pleasant the teeming
Underbelly of the city populace.
Throwing my core to a distant can,

My mark slightly altered by the wind,
My vessel struck the personage
Nearest to the receptacle.
Panicked I ran to
Investigate the
Manner of health in the recipient,
And turned towards me the
Face of
My love.
Glowing in the streetlamp light,
Her angry demeanour commanded
Legitimacy!
And, love-struck, I admitted
The deed and apologized for my miss.
Her angry frown turned round
At the cusp of my honesty.
She rose, and pulled the
Core from her jacket hood,
Whence it was lodged,
And a simultaneous laugh
Bound our love.
The promenade never had
Seen such a sight,
As two lovers converging
On the concrete square.

My eyes snap back to the present,
No time for remembrances now.
The pole centered in the arena,
I didn't have much time,
Nor now what to expect.
I pushed my way to the edge

Of the arena
Where a guard stood, asking my business.
"My love needs me like
the table needs coupes!"
I cried, and pushed my way
Into the arena.
The crowd erupted with a roar of
Protest, as I stumbled towards the center.
Suddenly a weight on my back!
The guard followed me
With a dagger to my throat,
Laying on top of me,
He whispered,
"Not on my watch, vagabond,"
and looked towards
Leif Erikson, who stood and
Surveyed the crowd.
A foreign chant begun,
A choice of slanted tongue
All were seeking my death
The guard was hard on top of me,
It was weird.
Murder was his arousal,
And it was also his business.
Leif Erikson held out his hand,
And the crowd silenced.
All eyes on him.

He stuck out his tongue
And spun around,
Licking his hand
And kicking his chair.

We all knew what that meant.
The guard grunted in disapproval of
The new order.
Took out he did his bamboo
Shackles, and dragged me to the
Flagpole.
And upon that pole he chained me
With panda food restraints,
Next to my love.
With my hands above my head,
I turned and saw her.
Behind the dust and
Newly given scars,
Were the eyes I had always adored.
As the ropes were pulled
And we were both lifted
Up, to the top of the pole,
I leaned over to her
And gently kissed her
Cheek.
Her eyes opened, and in a
Half conscious way,
She seemed to blink "I love you."
And I tenderly whispered in her
Ear,
As we dangled and dangled,
"I'm here, darling."
And she opened her eyes wider,
And then her mouth formed
The words: "I…will…always…"
And then unconscious.

I didn't know what would come.
Monsters from the deep,
Giant locusts,
Sexual advances from a gorilla.
All ran through my mind.
Some more than others.
The crowd was never louder than
When we dangled there,
Awaiting our fate.
In an instant, a giant green light
The size of ten robots
In the shape of an edgeless wonder,
Rose above the coliseum,
And, on its own pole,
Shot up thirty miles high
(an approximation. Science is
overrated. My feelings do more
for me than a ruler does.)
And a sound that shrilled
The ears of all
Emitted from every speaker.
After thirty seconds or so
It stopped.
And the light came down
And tucked itself back, away
Into its pocket.
And silence came once again.
Was that all?
Was the light and sound
Some sort of sensory torture?

No.

It was a beacon.
It was a call.
And soon whatever the green light
Had called,
Appeared in the distance.

At first it was merely
A black dot
In the air,
And as it came closer,
Two twig like shapes shot out of it,
Moving simultaneously up and down,
And as it came yet closer,
The body was mass.
Once the creature got close
Enough to distinct itself
To vision,
I closed my eyes,
To avoid fear for the upcoming resistance.
Hearing
Flap, flap, flap, flap.
Hush.
Awe.
Flap, flap, flap.
Blackness.
Wind and dry.
A boom.
And the ground shakes,
The pole tips back and forth.
The ground shakes in rhythm.
Giant steps?

Eyes still closed, resisting temptation.
Deny yourself now, reap the rewards later.
Rhythm rhythm
Till the last moment,
Don't think
Don't look.
Act.
Feeling hot breath,
Smells of death
A deep under-growling,
Sniff of giant vacuums.
Don't think.
Don't look.
Act.
With the bamboo tightly clad,
Eyes closed,
I pulled myself up, flipping
Backwards
Onto the top of the pole,
A balancing act.
Strength.
Break the bamboo!
Swan dive, eyes closed,
Down to the ground,
Flip at the last moment.
Absorb the impact.
Run.
Eyes open.
Towards the edge,
Running at full speed.
Pivot! Turn and face your enemy
With fuller advantage.

The comprehension of it overwhelms.
Four stories tall,
One wide at the hips,
Ten stories wide at the wing tips.
A dragon of immense proportions,
More terrifying than
Those of folklore.
A yellow belly deceived those
Who pout stock in the phrase "yellow bellied,"
For after the sight of this yellow belly,
Their stock would crash.
Yellow bleed into green
All around the scale-studded body,
Plates of hard steel and
Tetragonal obesity.
The wings dripped down from the
Two main shafts,
And the droplets
Became knives.
An unusual neck was its most fearsome
Facet.
Extending like a giant letter S,
It swirled around like an Amazonian tree trunk,
And itself was as large as his body.
The head was a goat's head,
With no fur or horns.
But had horns of ram
Swirling and pointing and princessing.
Round its neck, an unusual necklace
Of body skulls and live virgins,
Who screamed for mercy

As they dangled and dangled.
Around one of its car sized toes
Wrapped a ring
Silver and Gothic,
Wrapping eagle fangs that grasped
A ruby jeweled diamond
A the center of which
Was the Declaration of Independence.
Hunched over the flagpole
My love in danger,
The dragon reached high in the air,
But before it could strike down,
I shouted a distraction-insult:
"You there! Tectonic wonder!
I spit in the milk of your mother!
Unhand my love, or I shall
Rip you apart
With my bare hands!"
The dragon turned and snarled,
Its subway-neck cricking and cracking
Its long tail swung and
Snapped!
In the air as it turned,
A hundred yards away,
He opened his mouth,
And there was new light.
In a second I felt the heat,
And my dive narrowly escaped
The fire train that whizzed by.
Charred were my clothes,
Sunburned my skin.
And yet I stood,

My fist in the air, shouting,
"Bella Lostimon Fido Spira!"
And from my magic words,
The clouds opened up, and
Lightening struck my clenched
Fist.
The celestial charging blasted
My body against the
Coliseum wall,
And I laid unconscious.
The audience laughed, and
Leif Erikson leaned forward in his chair,
To see my "dead" body.
The Dragon laughed, as well,
Cackling a smoky bellow,
And left the flagpole to
Investigate the nature beaten, burned man.
It approached me, and I could
Feel the ground
In the darkness.
Then the crowd became
Audible.
Sight!
Eyes closed!
Let him come.
The dragon picked me up, its dry,
Scaly claws,
Loosely gripping my limp body.
I am an actor!
And as a child plays a game,
The dragon flung me in the air,
Higher than ten coliseums.

Passing the clouds as mist,
My apex reached,
I gently fell back.
When I was back in sight,
The dragon positioned himself
Under me,
His jaws ready to receive
His falling food.
His eyes closed, his tongue rolling out,
He eagerly awaited.
As I fell,
The crowd thought it was all over,
And some looked away,
Afraid of mortal gore.
But the electricity surged within me
And I grew from within.
Bursting out the sides of me,
Splitting my skin with pain,
Shot out,
Forty foot steel airplane wings,
And from them sprung eight jet engines,
And I clenched my fists
Like Superman
And flew from the snap of
The dragon's jaws,
Speeding out of the coliseum,
At the speed of sound,
Cold were the clouds as they seemed to play
With me,
And I was miles away before I could
Turn back.
My goggles on, I sped back,

And felt my love
Pound
In my chest.
I approached the coliseum,
And before my thoughts
Were there,
The dragon shot up towards my line
Of sight
And floated in front of me,
Hovering over the coliseum,
And without hesitation he flew backwards,
Getting room to charge
Like the pull of a slingshot
And then charged.
We were to meet
Directly above the coliseum,
Above all,
Including my unconscious love.
It was man/machine vs. dragon.
Faster, faster.
Goggles pressing hard.
Ahead, a pillar of fire shot towards me.
He was using unfair advantages,
From deep with me came
An impulse
I had never felt before.
I opened my mouth,
And automatically out came
Shards of ice
That shot faster than I was going.
It was like the snows of Kilamanjaro
On weather steroids.

The two forces met before we did,
And upon contact
Formed a philosophy
That spread over the whole world
And deceived many.
Our forces equal,
We charged on,
And me above the coliseum.
The dragon dodged at the
Last second,
Grabbing onto my left wing.
The weight pulled me left,
And we circled round the perimater
At the speed
Of a half-shout.
The G-forces were extreme
And I was glad for my goggles.
The dragon, his claws on
The end of the wing,
Was hanging on for dear life,
And our counter clockwise dance
Astounded the crowd.
But the dragon held on, and
Started to climb.
There was nothing to be done.
Once he reached my center,
It would be all over.
So I called to my love,
Screaming for her to awake.
It was I who needed help now.
No answer.
The dragon clawed close,

And as he came closer,
The weight shifted, and our
Circle became wider.
I was helpless,
And we were circling farther
And farther outside the stadium.
Again I called.
Nothing.
The dragon was now almost at my
Body.
He drew back his serpent head,
Like a cobra waiting to strike,
And jabbed,
Missing my head by a yard.
He needed more ground.
So he clawed another step,
And just as he cocked his head
Back for another go,
I heard her.
The sound of broken chairs,
The awed vocalization of the crowd,
And a boom.
My love boomed up from the stadium,
And explosion of smoke
From under her feet.
And the dragon and I
Spinning round her like a tethered ball,
Both looked at the angelic creature,
Poised with her hands out,
She was a letter T with a face.
And her eyes closed,
And as she levitated in her majesty.

And began to rotate.
The dragon and I were
Entranced,
And magic urged us not to look away.
She turned with us in unison,
Always facing us.
But soon she began to get ahead,
And would face us twice in one of our rotations
And three
And four,
And ten.
And the smoke under her
Turned, too.
And she was a vortex.
And then she turned on her side,
Slowly,
Still spinning,
And her head pointed towards
The east
And brought her arms
Towards her chest,
Her clenched fists no longer visible
In the horizontal blur.
And from her head,
A beam of light, brighter
Than the sun,
Emitted from her as a flashlight,
And the light stretched
To the horizon
And when I and the dragon
First passed through the light
Nothing happened.

The second, nothing.
But the third time
The dragon gasped.
And with every time
We passed the light,
The dragon became shorter of breath,
And soon had to clutch
Its throat, releasing its
Grip from my wings,
And he fell towards the
Coliseum,
Landing in the center arena, choking.
And I, free of weight,
Shot straight towards the
East, the beam of light
Pushing me forward
And reinforcing me.
But a new weight was
On my back.
Gentle arms clasped around my neck.

The sweet aroma of vanilla,
Soft hair dangling in front of my face,
And a cheek like a pillow next to mine,
As softly in my ear, soothing whisper:
"I knew you'd come, my love."
And her beam of light
Was one inside me,
And we were together again
And all the memories were
Welcome inside my familiarity,
And I soared to the horizon,

Until she said,
"Circle back, my love. We have
one more mission."
And so I turned,
Until the stadium was in line.
As we approached,
My love and I talked of
Past benches, waterfalls, and
Laughter.
And as we got closer,
I asked my love,
"What are we to do?"
And she said, "We must
Bomb the coliseum."
And I was startled.
"Darling, you are saved. Why must
they all die? The deed is done."
And her soft grip tightened,
Her smell became putrid,
And her voice harsh, as she snapped,
"They must die, now!"
and I thought of everyone
Leif Erikson, the guard,
The women, the children, the dragon.
"Why must they all die?"
My love answered,
"This is a test. If you do not
bomb them, I will leave you again."

And time almost stopped as the bomb dropped.
The dragon choking still,
Leif Erikson licking the ground,

The guard writing a song,
The women singing,
The children sleeping,
And as my love and I left them
All behind us, the bomb executed.
The brightness consumed the Earth
And shaking shockwave
Split the grounds
For miles,
And no one was anymore,
Save for the two of us.
And she said,
"Well done, my love."
And she smiled curiously.
And she slipped away
Behind me
Floating behind,
And I felt a heat,
The beam was now hate and revenge,
And I began to choke,
My wings disappeared,
And I hit the ground hard,
Rolling on cracked sand for miles.

My love nowhere to be seen,
My body broken,
My mouth full of sand,
And choking,
I lay here
Thinking about the walk, and the stadium.
I can't move. I can't speak.
My love… where have you gone?

And above me the vultures circle.
A new age will begin
After they peck away my remains,
My love the master,
And the birds her servants,
And they will peck away everyone
And peck away each other
Until she takes away their wings.
And she is never satisfied.
They are next to me, now.

I will get my love back, one day.

Outro.

A tattered collection of yellowed pages,
Thoughts concocted from unknown sages,
Here and there lie roots and reasons,
Oddly, evenly, ordered seasons.
But through A and B the mind rages.

The legend is real, or the stories are not,
The centered one will never be forgot,
Something to do, something to be,
Somewhere to go, something to see,
A pen to waste, and a mind to rot.

A finished page, a smiling turn,
Letting the past quickly burn,
A hilltop seat in the heavenly places,
Gently looking at uplifting faces,
Towards the new I yearn.

The hidden message, the masked sigh,
The hopeful wish that will never die,
The fencing distance and I with my sword,
The ignorant dreams I can't afford,
Reaching south as time goes by.

Holding my breath for the oncoming day,
Hoping for circumstance to turn my way,
Being busied with bills, school, and the rest,
Always giving my honest best,
My mind soaring on the fray.

So much to do.
And while I wait,
I go to.

-JL